Copyright © 2024
By Steven Sykes

ISBN: 9798340557667

Printed in the United States of America

All rights reserved solely by the author. The author guarantees all contents are original except where credit is attributed and does not infringe upon the legal rights of any other person or work. No part of this book may be reproduced in any form without the permission of the author.

All Scripture references are from the Authorized King James Bible.

BSALT Publications
Deming, New Mexico
First Edition

Table of Contents

LESSON ONE
The Importance of Soul-winning *1*

LESSON TWO
Man's Condition As A Sinner *9*

LESSON THREE
The Gospel Must Be Communicated *15*

LESSON FOUR
The Command of Personal Soul-Winning *25*

LESSON FIVE
What is the Gospel Message? *33*

LESSON SIX
Preparing Yourself Outwardly *43*

LESSON SEVEN:
Preparing Yourself Inwardly *51*

LESSON EIGHT
STEALTH In Soul-Winning *63*

LESSON ONE

The Importance of Soul-winning

"The Great Commission is not an option to be considered; it is a command to be obeyed."

- Hudson Taylor
(Missionary to China)

Introduction

Put your ear to the Bible and listen, look, and see on its pages its instructions to tell others about the gospel of the Lord Jesus Christ and to earnestly share the greatest news this world needs to hear.

We have a compelling reason to share the gospel in every corner of the world and every corner of our community. Every individual who leaves this world without salvation finds themselves in immediate and eternal torment.

1. The **g o s p e l** is the most important message in the Bible.

    A. The gospel addresses the greatest **n e e d** of humanity (reconciliation with God).

    B. The gospel applies **p e r s o n a l l y** to every individual (because all have sinned).

    C. The gospel answers man's greatest **q u e s t i o n** (what happens after you die?).

2. Unfortunately, the most important message in the Bible is so often the most **n e g l e c t e d** one that is supposed to be shared with others.

What the Bible Teaches
about Soul-winning

Proverbs 11:30 – *"The fruit of the righteous is a tree of life; and he that winneth souls is wise."*

» This verse teaches two aspects of soul-winning. It is **w i s e** to win souls, and it **t a k e s w i s d o m** to win souls. The wisdom needed to win souls comes from the Word of God, the source of wisdom, and not man's wisdom.

Psalms 126:5-6 – *"They that sow in tears shall reap in joy. He that goeth forth and weepeth, bearing precious seed, shall doubtless come again with rejoicing, bringing his sheaves with him."*

» Soul-winning requires a real, true **burden** and desire for those who are lost. Success is based largely upon **tears**.

Mark 16:15 – *"…Go ye into all the world, and preach the Gospel to every creature."*

» This verse reveals the **magnitude** of the task and responsibility.

Acts 20:20, 21 – *"And how I kept back nothing that was profitable unto you, but have shewed you, and have taught you publickly, and from house to house, Testifying both to the Jews, and also to the Greeks, repentance toward God, and faith toward our Lord Jesus Christ."*

» These verses describe how we are to witness. It is **personal** for the Christian, **profitable** to the listener, and from "house to house."

John 1:40-41 – *"One of the two which heard John speak, and followed him, was Andrew, Simon Peter's brother. He first findeth his own brother Simon, and saith unto him, We have found the Messias, which is, being interpreted, the Christ."*

John 1:43, 45 – *"The day following Jesus would go forth into Galilee, and findeth Philip, and saith unto him, Follow me. Philip findeth Nathanael, and saith unto him, We have found him, of whom Moses in the law, and the prophets, did write, Jesus of Nazareth, the son of Joseph."*

» These verses teach the personal **w i t n e s s** of the believer to all the unsaved.

Our Commitment & Obligation as a Christian:

(The "WHY" of Soul winning) It is not always easy; it is not always comfortable. We do not necessarily know what is going on in a person's heart or life when we witness to them. We have an enemy who wants to hinder our efforts to share the gospel.

1. We are obligated by the **c r o s s** of Christ.

Hebrews 12:3 – *"For consider him that endured such contradiction of sinners against himself, lest ye be wearied and faint in your minds."*

» The **s u f f e r i n g** of Christ should motivate the believer to become a soul-winner.

2. We are obligated by the **command** of Christ.

   » The believer is obligated to be obedient to Christ. Soul-winning is **not** an option. If you are not a soul-winner, you are in **disobedience**.

3. We are obligated by the **change** the gospel had on you as a believer.

   » There was a time when the gospel did not mean anything to you, but when someone brought you the gospel message, you at some point received it to be the Word of God, and responded to the gospel, you got saved. The gospel took on a whole new meaning and importance, and you had a new appreciation of God for it.

4. We are obligated by the **consequences** of judgment.

Ezekiel 18:20 —"The soul that sinneth, it shall die"

Romans 6:23 – "The wages of sin is death"

Hebrews 9:27 – "And as it is appointed unto men once to die, but after this the judgment:"

Revelation 20:15 – "And whosoever was not found written in the book of life was cast into the lake of fire"

Ezekiel 33:1–6 – "Again the word of the LORD came unto me, saying,

Son of man, speak to the children of thy people, and say unto them, When I bring the sword upon a land, if the people of the land take a man of their coasts, and set him for their watchman:

If when he seeth the sword come upon the land, he blow the trumpet, and warn the people;

Then whosoever heareth the sound of the trumpet, and taketh not warning; if the sword come, and take him away, his blood shall be upon his own head.

He heard the sound of the trumpet, and took not warning; his blood shall be upon him. But he that taketh warning shall deliver his soul.

But if the watchman **see the sword come**, and blow not the trumpet, and the people be not warned; if the sword come, and take any person from among them, he is taken away in his iniquity; but his blood will I require at the watchman's hand."

5. We are obligated to the **s i n n e r** .

Romans 1:14-16 – "I am debtor both to the Greeks, and to the Barbarians; both to the wise, and to the unwise.

So, as much as in me is, I am ready to preach the gospel to you that are at Rome also.

For I am not ashamed of the gospel of Christ: for it is the power of God unto salvation to every one that believeth; to the Jew first, and also to the Greek."

Points To Ponder and Discuss

1. Every human being is a sinner and is already condemned without Jesus Christ.

2. Every individual who dies without salvation will immediately and eternally be in torment with no possibility of salvation.

3. It is the personal responsibility of every born-again believer to share the gospel of Jesus Christ with the lost.

4. We are commanded to share the gospel! We should be compelled to share the gospel!

5. The gospel is the most important message in the Bible, and salvation is the greatest need of mankind.

LESSON TWO

Man's Condition As A Sinner

Showing People They Are Lost Is The First Hurdle We Must Overcome

1. We must remember that part of soul-winning is communicating to the world and the individual that everyone needs a Savior because of our **sinful condition**. There is no way around this.

2. God's Word lays out very clearly our condition of being sinners. We must understand as Christians and soul winners that ALL PEOPLE ARE **ALREADY** CONDEMNED AS SINNERS.

3. You are going to have some people that you witness to who think they are "good" people in a lot of different ways.

A. Some will not see themselves as <u>**condemned**</u> sinners.

B. People usually see <u>**themselves**</u> as trying to do right and generally good people, even when they are not.

The Concept Illustrated

<u>True Example from Bro. Steven Sykes; Founder of BSALT and Church Planter in New Mexico:</u>

Several years ago we were doing a soul-winning campaign with a church in some apartment buildings. I witnessed to a young single mother trying to raise her two kids.

I asked her if she would go to heaven if something happened to her and she died. She very quickly replied that she would. I asked her how she knew for sure she would go to heaven.

Her reply, "Because I'm a good mom, and I am trying hard to raise my kids."

Herein lies the difficulty. I could tell that this young lady was indeed trying hard to raise her children on her own and be a good mother. But the truth, God's Word, clearly shows us that her efforts to be a good mother will not give her salvation and forgiveness of sin.

I told this young lady that I appreciated her effort and commitment to be a good mother. I did not want to take that away from her, but I took some time and shared with her some of the verses above to help her understand that trying to be a good mother or any "good work" is not going to give her salvation.

I illustrated this for her by speaking of someone getting a speeding ticket. "If you get a speeding ticket, do you have to go to court and stand before the judge?" "Yes," she said. I then said, "What do you think the judge would say if you told the judge that most of the time you do not speed, that most of the time you obey the speeding laws, and that your good driving should outweigh breaking the law by speeding?" I went on to tell her that the judge would likely tell her, "You are not here to stand before me for what you did right. You are here for me to judge what you did wrong, and how you broke the law."

This helped her better understand her situation, and that our righteousness can never be a substitute for our sin or reconcile us to God.

I went on to tell her that a relationship with the Lord Jesus Christ is what is needed in her life for the forgiveness of sin and salvation.

After spending time showing her the truth of God's Word, this young lady trusted the Lord Jesus Christ to be her Saviour.

4. The first step to being a good soul winner is to recognize these **false** perceptions and tendencies to have our **own righteousness** and to give every individual the truth from God's Word.

What the Bible Teaches
About Man's Sinful Condition

There are many verses you can share with someone that will clearly show them our condition of being sinners.

Romans 3:23 "For **all** have **sinned**, and come short of the glory of God;"

1 John 1:8 "If we say that we have no sin, we **deceive** ourselves, and the truth is not in us."

Ecclesiastes 7:20 "For there is not a just man upon earth, that doeth good, and **sinneth not**."

Psalm 51:5 "Behold, I was shapen in iniquity, and in **sin** did my mother conceive me."

Jeremiah 17:9 "The heart is deceitful above all things, and desperately **wicked**: who can know it?"

Romans 5:12 "Wherefore, as by one man sin entered into the world, and death by sin; and so death passed upon all men, for that **all** have sinned."

Galatians 3:22 "But the scripture hath concluded all <u>u n d e r</u> sin, that the promise by faith of Jesus Christ might be given to them that believe."

Romans 3:10 "As it is written, There is <u>**n o n e**</u> righteous, no, not one:"

Psalm 130:3-4 "If thou, Lord, shouldest mark iniquities, O Lord, who shall stand? But there is forgiveness with thee, that thou mayest be feared."

1 Timothy 1:15 "This is a faithful saying, and worthy of all acceptation, that Christ Jesus came into the world to save <u>**s i n n e r s**</u>; of whom I am chief."

The Apostle Paul considered himself the chief of sinners. It is in the Bible so it must be true. Before Paul got saved he was a religiously "good man," a Pharisee of Pharisees, who earnestly tried to keep the Old Testament Law. In our eyes, we would say he was a "good man" (Philippians 3:4-9).

Teacher's Notes:

Open up a discussion about instances students have come across people who were genuinely convinced of their own goodness. What other ways can you illustrate to a person who is "trying their best" that they are sinful by nature?

Points To Ponder and Discuss

1. Everyone is a sinner in need of salvation only through Jesus Christ.

2. The first hurdle to overcome is showing the person to whom we are witnessing, their sinful condition.

3. It is wrong to let them tell you a self-righteous perception of salvation or any wrong, unbiblical means of salvation and not tell them the truth of God's Word.

4. Discuss the verses that clearly show man's sin.

5. Even Paul, a religiously superior man, was sinful in his nature.

LESSON THREE

The Gospel Must Be Communicated

"The Gospel is not good advice to be obeyed, it is good news to be believed.

Harry Ironside

"The gospel is so simple that small children can understand it, and it is so profound that studies by the wisest theologians will never exhaust its riches."

Charles Hodge

"I lived in fear most of my childhood. My dad was a monster, and I realized if the gospel could change him, the gospel can change anybody."

Anonymous

Rom 1:16 "For I am not **ashamed** of the gospel of Christ: for it is the power of God unto salvation to **everyone** that believeth; to the Jew first, and also to the Greek.

15

Communicating the Gospel Is The Second Hurdle That We Must Overcome

1. You will find the phrase "preach the gospel" **eleven** times in the New Testament. One of the most compelling Scriptures is:

   A. *Mark 16:15* "And he said unto them, Go ye into all the world, and preach the gospel to every creature."

   B. This is the **command** of our Lord Jesus Christ.

2. This command by our Lord Jesus Christ is the **basis** for:

   A. Sending and supporting **missionaries**.

   B. Supporting and involvement in church **planting**.

   C. Missionary Helps Ministries.

   D. Church **outreach** programs.

   E. Personal **soul-winning**.

3. It should be important to every Christian and every church to support and participate in all the above. The overall goal is to:

    A. Evangelize

    B. Baptize

    C. Stabilize

"God wants every creature to have a preacher."
Stinnett Ballew

Stinnett Ballew used to say:

- In order for a sinner to be saved, he/she must "call upon the name of the Lord" for salvation. (Romans 10:13).

- In order for him to call upon the name of the Lord, he must believe (Romans 10:14).

- In order for him to believe, he must first hear (v. 14).

- In order for him to hear, there must be a preacher. (v. 14).

- In order for him to preach, he first must be sent (**Romans 10:15**).

- I am glad that God is still calling preachers to preach, missionaries to go, and church planters to start churches!

4. We are not all called to be preachers, missionaries, church planters, etc., but we can all participate in the "SENDING," "HELPING," "ENCOURAGING," and "PARTNERSHIP" of God called men and their families.

Philippians 4:15-16 *"Now ye Philippians know also, that in the beginning of the gospel, when I departed from Macedonia, no church communicated with me as concerning giving and receiving, but ye only. For even in Thessalonica ye sent once and again unto my necessity."*

» The church in Philippi provided **financial support** to Paul during his missionary journeys. They sent financial offerings to help him with his needs as he labored to share the gospel.

» ***2 Corinthians 1:11***: We can provide **prayer support**.

» ***Acts 18:2-3***: We can provide **shelter**, **hospitality**, and extend **help**.

» Can participate with **special** needs.

» Can participate in **mission's** trips to help.

» Can help with **encouragement** (send a card, make a call, send a text).

Class Discussion

Open a class discussion on possible ways individual church members can participate in supporting the preaching of the Gospel. What ways can Churches be involved?

5. We ALL, every born-again believer can:

   A. We can all be involved in **local church outreach**.

Here are some united efforts with your church to reach the lost in your area.

- Outreach program
- Visitation
- Food pantry
- Soup kitchen or community meals
- Men/Women's home
- Senior citizen outreach (Nursing homes)
- Hospital outreach
- Disaster relief
- Community garden
- Addictions programs
- Prison ministries
- Mentorship programs

   B. What are some other church ministries that can **reach** the lost in your community?

   C. Your **pastor** can discuss with you the vision and local church outreach ministries and how you can get involved.

   1.) Keep in mind most churches cannot do **everything**.

   2.) But every church should do **something**.

3.) Discuss with your pastor about participation.

    a.) He will discuss with you the ministries.

    b.) He will discuss with you your spiritual gifts.

    c.) He will make recommendations of involvement.

4.) Involvement will help you become a better soulwinner.

5.) Involvement is serving the Lord.

6.) God will grow your life and use you for His will through involvement.

7.) Get involved, be committed, learn and grow, and bear much fruit!!

8.) Share stories and encourage other Christians to get involved.

Keep in mind the devil will fight against you serving the Lord. The flesh will want to do other things, and you must not allow worldliness to substitute serving the Lord.

6. We should all be involved in <u>**personal soulwinning**</u>.

Fighting the Enemy
More Hurdles To Overcome

1. A **Hidden** Message

2 Corinthians 4:3-5 *"But if our gospel be hid, it is hid to them that are lost: In whom the god of this world hath blinded the minds of them which believe not, lest the light of the glorious gospel of Christ, who is the image of God, should shine unto them. For we preach not ourselves, but Christ Jesus the Lord; and ourselves your servants for Jesus' sake.*

2. Darkness

   A. The world in general does not **know** the gospel.

   B. The world in general has been **blinded** by Satan from the light of the gospel. Satan has **darkened** the minds of the lost.

   C. Satan has put many **obstacles** between the lost and the gospel:

   » pleasures
   » possessions
   » pride
   » people
   » products
   » philosophies
   » perceptions

3. Distraction

   A. Another reason the gospel is hidden from the lost is because many Christians do not provide the gospel to the unsaved. Many Christians do not P. REACH the gospel. WHY?

   - » unconcerned
   - » apathy
   - » indifference
   - » fear
   - » sin
   - » entanglements
   - » worldly distractions
   - » overreliance on personal abilities

   B. Many times, **we fail to follow up**. We **m u s t c o n t i n u e** to reach out to those that we have shared the gospel with previously.

   » Sometimes Christians do not **f o l l o w** up. A Soul-winner must continue to reach after the initial discussion.

4. Discipline is **N e e d e d** !

Points To Ponder and Discuss:

1. "Preach the gospel" phrase said eleven times in the Bible. The gospel must be communicated.

2. This command should be important to every Christian and church.

3. The Lord's command is the basis for:

    A. Sending and supporting missionaries.

    B. Supporting and involvement in church planting.

    C. Missionary Helps Ministries.

    D. Church outreach programs.

    E. Personal soulwinning.

4. It is important that every church (Christians) participate in evangelizing, baptizing, and stabilizing unsaved individuals.

5. Not everyone is called to preach, but we ALL are commanded to "preach the gospel." Every Christian should participate by supporting missions and church planting financially, prayerfully, and extending help.

6. Get involved in local church outreach. Talk to your pastor and discuss with him how you can get involved.

7. Every born-again believer should share the gospel with those they encounter (family, friends, co-workers, neighbors, strangers, and people in their daily lives).

8. Personal soulwinning should become a part of who you are and your lifestyle.

9. We have some hurdles to overcome in presenting and providing the gospel:

    A. The world is in darkness.

    B. Many Christians are distracted.

    C. Discipline to present and provide the gospel is needed.

LESSON FOUR

The Command of Personal Soul-Winning

"The only alternative to soul winning is disobedience to Christ."

Curtis Hutson

"A Christian is to be a soul winner."

Tom Malone

"One soul won to Christ is better than a thousand merely moralized and still sleeping in their sins."

Charles Spurgeon

"Personal soul winning is the greatest work to which any Christian can address himself."

R.A. Torrey

Let us go back to our great commission and instruction from our Lord Jesus Christ.

Mark 16:15 *"And he said unto them,* **Go** *ye into all the world, and* **preach** *the gospel to every creature."*

What the Bible Teaches
About Personal Soul-winning

Proverbs 11:30 *"The fruit of the righteous is a tree of life,* **and he that winneth souls is wise.***"*

» This verse teaches that a **righteous** person will bear fruit. Not bearing fruit shows a lack of doing the right things!

2 Corinthians 5:20 *"Now then we are* **ambassadors** *for Christ."*

Acts 1:8 *"But ye shall receive power, after that the Holy Ghost is come upon you: and* **ye shall be witnesses** *unto me both in Jerusalem, and in all Judaea, and in Samaria, and unto the uttermost part of the earth."*

*"Preaching the Gospel is something every disciple is **expected** to major in."*

Harry Ironside

» In some things, God uses God-called preachers (missionaries, church planting, evangelists, etc.). But in the context of our instructions in this verse, **every** born-again believer **should** be involved.

» Definition: preach- to **proclaim**, announce **publicly**, publish, to declare.

» Every Christian is responsible for **p r o c l a i m i n g** the gospel of Jesus Christ. Your requirement is to be saved.

1. Because it is a command, you do not have to **w a i t** to feel "led" to share the gospel.

Teacher's Illustration

If you have children or employees, you are likely able to insert a personal illustration that your class could identify with. The illustration should convey that obedience to authority is expected immediately. If you'd like, you can use the following illustration that's been provided:

If I instruct my son to take out the trash before dark, he is expected to do it before dark. What if my son said, "Dad I am waiting until I feel led to take out the trash." Or if my son said, "Dad I am waiting for just the right time to take out the trash," and he delays taking it out day after day. Many Christians do this very thing with the Lord's command to proclaim the gospel.

2. "PREACH THE GOSPEL" is for EACH of us. The word PREACH contains the word EACH. Great reminder to each of us to preach the Gospel.

Acronym #1

P **Personally. REACH**
REACH Personally REACH the lost with the gospel.

Acronym #2

P **Proclaim**
Proclaim the gospel to those around you. Ex. co-workers, family, neighbors, friends, places you go and people you see, strangers.

R **Receptive**
When you are talking to people, be receptive and <u>l i s t e n</u>. You do not at this point have to "Fix" everything they say. Be a good listener. Be friendly. Build a relationship.

E **Engage**
<u>E n g a g e</u> in the conversation with the gospel. Sometimes Christians will talk to people about all kinds of things except the gospel and salvation. We must engage people with the gospel

A **Authentic**
When you share the gospel, it must be <u>g e n u i n e</u>, heartfelt, and come from one who values the gospel. Soul-winning requires a real, true burden and desire for those who are lost. Success is based largely upon <u>t e a r s</u> (mentioned in an earlier lesson).

Psalms 126:5-6 – *"They that sow in tears shall reap in joy. He that goeth forth and weepeth, bearing precious seed, shall doubtless come again with rejoicing, bringing his sheaves with him."*

C **Christ Jesus**
We must lift Him up; not ourselves, not what we have done. We must decrease. Lift up the name of **J e s u s**. Make the gospel message all about what HE has done to save us.

H **Help and Hope**
Leave the one you are witnessing to with HELP and **H O P E** in Jesus Christ.

3. Leave them with a **p e r s o n a l** testimony of how the Lord has helped you.

   A. Mention the benefits of having a relationship with the Lord.

   - » Sins are forgiven
   - » peace with God
   - » eternal life
   - » purpose and meaning in life
   - » guidance and wisdom
   - » help in challenging times
   - » victory over the world
   - » a promised home in heaven with the Lord
   - » Etc. Etc. – We could spend hours talking about the benefits of being saved

   B. At this point, **we leave them with a question mark, not an exclamation mark.** We never want to **f o r c e** or push someone into a profession.

C. After discussing the gospel with them, let them take the next step.

1.) "John," if you want to be saved, I will be glad to answer any questions you may have.

2.) "Jill," is there any reason you would not want to be saved today?

3.) "Jerry," what are your thoughts on praying and asking the Lord to forgive you of your sins and save you?

4.) "Jaime," would you like to pray and ask the Lord to save you?

D. Always let them take the next step; never push or pull a profession. It must come from their heart, not yours.

E. Sometimes going from the P in P.R.E.A.C.H. to the H may take minutes, hours, days, or years. Do not rush the lost person.

F. Remember, you are sharing the gospel from the outward; the Holy Spirit is working from the inward of their heart. Do not rush! **Better to be R E A L than RUSHED!**

Points To Ponder and Discuss:

1. It is the responsibility of every Christian to "Preach the gospel"- To proclaim, announce publicly and publish, to declare.

2. You do not have to wait to feel "led" to share the gospel.

3. Personally Reach —— P. REACH.

4. P- Proclaim the gospel

5. R- Receptive; listen. You do not have to fix what they believe at this point. Be friendly. Be a good listener. Build a relationship.

6. E- Engage with the gospel.

7. A-Be authentic. Be genuine from your heart of experience with the gospel.

8. C- Christ, it is all about HIM.

9. H- Leave the one you are witnessing to with Hope and help from the Lord.

10. Leave the lost person you are witnessing with a question mark, not an exclamation mark. Never push salvation. Remember, it must come from their heart, not yours.

11. Sometimes going from the P in P.R.E.A.C.H. to the H may take minutes, hours, days, or years. Do not rush the lost person. It is more important for salvation to be REAL than RUSHED.

12. Remember, you are sharing the gospel from the outward; the Holy Spirit is working from the inward of their heart. Let God bring them to the place of salvation.

LESSON FIVE

What is the Gospel Message?

"Gentlemen, This Is A Football!"

In July 1961, Vince Lombardi kicked off the first day of training camp for the thirty-eight players on his Green Bay Packers football team. The prior season had ended in a heartbreaking loss to the Philadelphia Eagles after blowing a lead in the fourth quarter of the NFL Championship Game.

When the players came in to start training camp, they expected to immediately begin where they left off and work on ways to advance their game and learn fancy new ways to win the championship in the new season. When they sat down and began, Vince Lombardi held up a football and said, **"Gentlemen, this is a football!"**

He then had everyone open their playbooks and start on page one where they began to go over the fundamentals of football – blocking, tackling, throwing, catching, etc. That was clearly not what they expected as players who were at the top of their game.

These focused fundamentals allowed them to win the NFL Championship that season 37-0 against the New York Giants. Vince Lombardi went on to win five NFL Championships in seven years. He never coached a team with a losing season after that and never lost a playoff game again.

It is of utmost importance to focus on the fundamentals and the basics.

Fundamentals We Need To Focus On

1. Christians, this is God's Holy Word.

2. **The g r e a t e s t man** in the Bible is Jesus Christ.

    A. He is the Savior of the world.

    B. He is God who became man.

    C. He is the ONLY way to be saved from your sins. He is THE way, THE truth, THE life.

- D. He is the Son of God.
- E. Neither is there salvation in any other (**Acts 4:12**).
- F. There is ONE mediator between God and men, the man Christ Jesus (**1 Tim 2:5**).

3. The **greatest m e s s a g e** in the Bible is **the gospel of the Lord Jesus Christ.**

    - A. Broadly, it is the **w h o l e** of Scripture.
    - B. **In summary**, it is the good news that Jesus Christ, the Son of God came into the world to pay the sin debt of mankind. Jesus was born of a virgin, completely sinless. He was crucified, shed his blood on the cross at "Calvary," and died. After Jesus' death on the cross on the third day Jesus arose alive from the tomb. Because of His atonement and sacrifice for our sins, we can be saved from our sins by repentance and putting our faith in the Lord Jesus Christ. The message of the gospel is that through Jesus Christ we can have redemption and justification therefore being reconciled to God.

1 Corinthians 15:3-4 "For I delivered unto you first of all that which I also received, how that Christ died for our sins according to the scriptures; And that he was buried, and that he rose again the third day according to the scriptures:

C. We do not have to push, pump, pad, paint, sell, prop it up, popularize it, try to make it pretty, provoke people with it, or puff it up.

D. The gospel is the **p o w e r** of God. It does not need our power; we just present it, declare it, and provide it to the lost.

A Principle We Should Know

God uses things we do understand to help us understand truths we may not understand.

1. Soul winning is likened to **f i s h i n g** in the Bible.

Matthew 4:19 – *"Follow me and I* **w i l l** *make you fishers of men."*

   A. A fisherman goes where the fish **a r e**.

   B. A fisherman must go **f i s h i n g** to catch fish.

   C. You cannot clean a fish until you **c a t c h** a fish.

   D. A fisherman must be **p a t i e n t**.

   E. A fisherman **m u s t** keep trying.

- F. A fisherman cannot let winds or waves **s t o p** him from fishing.

- G. A fish may put up a **f i g h t**!

2. Soul winning is likened to **f a r m i n g** in the Bible.

Psalm 126:6 – *"He that goeth forth and weepeth, bearing precious seed, shall doubtless come again with rejoicing, bringing his sheaves with him."*

1 Corinthians 3:6-8 *"I have planted, Apollos watered; but God gave the increase. So then neither is he that planteth any thing, neither he that watereth; but God that giveth the increase. Now he that planteth and he that watereth are one: and every man shall receive his own reward according to his own labour.*

- A. Soil **c o n d i t i o n s** (the heart) have a lot to do with having a harvest (Mark 4).

- B. **P r e p a r a t i o n** of the soil must happen before the seed (the gospel) is received into the ground.

- C. Hardened soil must be **p l o w e d**. Just as the Holy Spirit is the axe head, the Holy Spirit is the plow. You and I cannot soften a heart, but God can.

- D. Clots in the soil **h i n d e r** the seed.

E. Sticks, stones, and stumps can **p r e v e n t** the seed from taking root.

F. God **w o r k s** in the hearts (soil) of people to receive the seed (the gospel).

G. **Planting of the seed** must happen **b e f o r e** there can be a harvest.

1.) We may plant individual seeds or use the **b r o a d c a s t** method.

2.) Planting takes **p e r s p i r a t i o n**.

3.) Planting takes **t i m e**.

4.) Planting takes **p r o t e c t i o n**. (Sometimes birds or other animals will steal the seed, so we need to replant.)

Teacher's Note

Before moving on with the lesson, take a minute to allow discussion of other ways that fishing or farming is like soulwinning.

H. Providing water is a requirement. **Watering the seed** (Apollos watered v. 6).

» The metaphor of "watering the seed" is often used to describe the process of nurturing and supporting someone's initial exposure to the gospel.

» Here are **eight practical ways to "water the seed"** based on biblical principles:

1.) Build Relationships with those who you are trying to win to Christ.

2.) Prayer- Pray regularly for those you are desiring to reach with the gospel.

3.) Listening- Take time to listen to concerns, questions, problems, and other things important to those you desire to reach (clots, sticks, stones, and stumps).

4.) Answering Questions- Be prepared to answer questions about your faith, the Bible, Christianity, etc. Providing good and well-thought-out answers will help remove obstacles for the person to get saved.

5.) Sharing Personal Testimonies- Sharing your own experiences of how the Lord has helped you and how the Bible impacted your life can help them relate and provide a real-life example of Christian faith.

6.) Providing Resources- Offer relevant materials such as a Bible, booklets, tracts, and other literature so that the person can learn and read about topics of interest (Be sure the materials are biblical and King James).

7.) **<u>Invite Them to Church</u>**- Invite the person to attend church with you. Be sure that when they come, you sit with them, show them around, and introduce them to the pastor and other Christians. Take them to lunch after church. Help them feel received and have an enjoyable time at church.

8.) **<u>Model Christian Faith</u>**- You should know that the people to whom you witness will be watching your life and how you respond to difficulties in life, challenges, and other things. They want to see if your Christianity is real and makes a difference in your life. Please know that as you live the Christian faith authentically and genuinely it can have a profound impact on those who are watching you. Let your light shine!

Please remember that when it comes to fishing or farming, it takes patience. Be patient with people. **<u>Do not give up.</u>**

Teacher's Illustration

If you have your own illustration of a person you have seen trust Christ after months or years of patiently waiting for God to "plow" and "water" their heart, share it with your students at this point in the lesson.

If you would like the following illustration is provided by Steven Sykes:

"I remember a young man years ago who started attending our services. He would observe and listen intently, but he always kept an arm's length distance away from allowing me to gain a closer friendship with him. I would talk to him about the gospel and salvation, but many times he told me that he was not ready to get saved or that he was thinking about it. For a year, I continued to pray for him and with him, give him materials, answer questions, share personal testimonies of what God had done in my life, and counsel him to help him with things that had happened in his life (clots, sticks, stones, and stumps). I never pushed him to get saved. It had to be from his heart and not mine. Much watering had been done for over a year since I first shared the gospel with him.

One day during the week, this young man stopped by the church and wanted to talk. He came into my office and said that he wanted to get saved. God had been working in his heart softening the soil, and the seed finally popped out with life. This young man bowed his head and trusted Christ for salvation. God gave the increase!"

Points To Ponder and Discuss:

1. The greatest man in the Bible is Jesus Christ. Make much of Jesus!

2. The greatest message in the Bible is the gospel of the Lord Jesus Christ.

3. You do not have to push, pump up, puff up, or prop up the gospel. The gospel is the power of God. It just needs to be presented and provided.

4. Soulwinning is likened to fishing and farming in the Bible.

    A. Patience is needed in fishing and farming.

    B. Fish must be caught before they are cleaned.

    C. Planting seeds can be done individually or by broadcast method.

    D. Seed must be watered. Review the Eight ways to water the seed.

    E. God gives the increase.

LESSON SIX

Preparing Yourself Outwardly

BSALT has shared the gospel with over 600,000 homes across twenty-five states. From years of experience, we want to share some practical advice when it comes to soulwinning and sharing the gospel door-to-door. This is by no means exhaustive, and we continue to learn. But we desire to be fishers of men. We know that the greatest need in the United States and the world is the gospel of the Lord Jesus Christ.

Matthew 28:18-20 – "And Jesus came and spake unto them, saying, All power is given unto me in heaven and in earth. Go ye therefore, and teach all nations, baptizing them in the name of the Father, and of the Son, and of the Holy Ghost: Teaching them to observe all things whatsoever I have commanded you: **and, lo, I am with you alway**, even unto the end of the world. Amen."

Acts 1:8 – "But ye shall receive power, after that **the Holy Ghost** is come upon you: and ye shall be witnesses unto me both in Jerusalem, and in all Judaea, and in Samaria, and unto the uttermost part of the earth."

1. **Soulwinning is a p a r t n e r s h i p**. You will never have to do it alone. God is at work helping both you and the recipient of the gospel.

   A. He helps you to share the gospel and to give an answer.

   B. He **c o n v i c t s** the recipient of the gospel and works to soften their heart to the gospel.

   C. The Holy Spirit will continue to work in the heart of the recipient long after you have finished proclaiming or providing the gospel.

2. We believe in **D i v i n e appointments**. Jesus waiting at the well for the Samaritan woman was a Divine appointment. But we should not just wait for a Divine appointment. We should always be ready to share the gospel, and we are commanded to share the gospel.

A Divine Appointment

Several years ago, while planting the church in Deming, NM, we had a lady coming through Deming on Interstate I-10. Her vehicle broke down as she was coming through our small town. She put her vehicle in the shop and had no other choice but to wait for it to be checked out and repaired. On Friday she called me and requested a ride to church for Sunday. She explained the situation, and we were glad to have her visit our church. On Saturday, she got the bad news. (Well, at that point she thought it was bad news). The repair shop said the transmission had to be rebuilt on her vehicle. They said it would take two weeks, and it was not a cheap repair.

On Sunday, she requested prayer for the situation and the needed money and was upset and frustrated. I prayed with her and mentioned to her that maybe God had her here in Deming, NM, for a reason and to not think that this was a bad situation.

Over the next two weeks, my wife and I gave her the gospel and watered the seed as much as we could. She came faithfully to the services because she said it helped her emotionally with the situation. Little did she realize what the Lord was doing.

In the last service she was with us at the end of the service she came forward and trusted Jesus Christ as her Savior. She had tears of joy and she realized that the reason God had her "stuck" in Deming, NM, was so she could hear the gospel and get saved. A couple of days later the vehicle was repaired; some of her family wired her some money to pay the expense, and she was ready to go.

On her way out of town, she stopped by the church and talked to my wife and me. She was so full of joy and gratitude for what the Lord had done in her life. We all prayed together and thanked the Lord for her Divine appointment in Deming, NM.

Time would fail me to tell you about the folks that have run out of gas in front of our church or stopped at our church weeping and broken needing prayer.

Always pray for and be on the lookout for Divine appointments.

3. Be **p r e p a r e d** to share the gospel.

   A. Until you are familiar with soul-winning Scripture, it is our advice to carry with you or in your vehicle a small New Testament Bible or tracts. You can also use a Bible app on your phone. You can use the New Testament or the tracts to share Scripture or give the tracts to people.

   B. If you are going with your church outreach group to knock on doors and personally invite the community or soul-winning in some other way in your community, be prepared. Before you go out with your church be sure to consider what material things you should take with you.

4. Our BSALT Team, except for the Scriptures, calls these things **t o o l s** .

A. A plumber has tools, an electrician has tools, and a doctor has tools. **<u>Soul winners should use tools.</u>**

1.) Tools make the job easier.

2.) Tools make the job more efficient.

3.) Tools can make the job more accurate.

4.) Tools can reduce labor intensity.

5.) Tools can increase output.

6.) Tools can increase the quality of a job well done.

The Concept Illustrated

In the early 2000's a Swiss man named Torben Frandsen recognized the need for a portable, cost-effective, easy-to-use water purification instrument. The result of his effort to develop this tool was called the LifeStraw, a compact, tube-shaped filter that could be used as a personal and portable device to filter out contaminants and make water safe to drink. The LifeStraw requires no batteries, electrical power, or additional chemicals or equipment.

The impact of the LifeStraw has been amazing, particularly in areas where clean and safe drinking water is limited. The LifeStraw has saved lives, been used in disaster relief, and allowed people in remote areas to have clean drinking water. The LifeStraw has received numerous awards and recognition. Many consider it to be a game-changer.

B. It goes to show you how developing soul-winning tools can make a substantial difference and **impact** on presenting and providing the gospel message.

C. We are **always** needing Christian volunteers who can help develop soul-winning tools to better present and provide the gospel message.

1.) Design materials such as tracts, literature, etc.

2.) Tech, Apps, or other electronic means.

3.) Through a sharing of ideas, input, and participation let us create or improve our tools to share the gospel.

4.) Please contact BSALT if you would like to get involved in this area.

D. Below is a list of tools that you should consider in preparation to go out soul-winning:

- » New Testament with relevant verses easily identified
- » Church tracts and/or church invitation cards
- » Clear bags if you are hanging a packet
- » John & Romans
- » Index cards or your phone to jot down prospect information
- » Church event invitations
- » Water and snacks
- » A partner or partners
- » An ink pen and notepad
- » Comfortable footwear
- » An app on your phone that you can use to share the gospel.
- » Weather-appropriate gear (sunscreen, umbrella, jacket, etc.)
- » A map or navigation app
- » Hand sanitizer
- » Church gift if applicable
- » Language translation app
- » Dog treats
- » Candy
- » Church bulletin or calendar

E. P r e p a r a t i o n before perspiration.

"By failing to prepare, you are preparing to fail."

Benjamin Franklin

Points To Ponder and Discuss:

1. Soul winning is a partnership. You will never do it alone. The Lord is always with you and will help you proclaim and provide the gospel.

2. The Holy Spirit convicts the sinner of sin and works in their heart long after a person has finished sharing the gospel.

3. Be prepared to share the gospel.

4. Tools make the job easier.

LESSON SEVEN:

Preparing Yourself Inwardly

Having all the soul-winning tools in the world is not going to be as beneficial as it could be unless you are spiritually prepared yourself.

Scripture Memorization

1. **Add Scripture:** Every Christian should add **Scripture** to memory.

    A. I know what you are thinking, "I don't have a good memory." "I have a hard time memorizing things." Memorization can be boring and difficult. YES!!!

    B. The goal is to retain God's Word in our heart.

Psalm 119:11 *"Thy word have I hid in mine heart, that I might not sin against thee."*

C. The word hide means to **s t o r e u p** in the mind and memory.

I agree with you that memorization is difficult and to simply memorize something may not "stick" very long. So, I have a better suggestion. Instead of "trying" to memorize Scripture, let us do all the things that will help us retain it in our hearts for the long haul:

1.) Start off by **p r a y i n g** and asking God to help you hide His Word in your heart.

2.) Secondly, choose some **meaningful Scriptures** that you really **w a n t** to retain in your mind and memory (the Romans Road to salvation).

3.) **R e a d repeatedly** those Scriptures and familiarize yourself with the words and order.

4.) **Write them down**. Write down by hand the Scriptures that you are wanting to retain. The act of **w r i t i n g** reinforces memory retention.

5.) Read the verses **aloud**. Hearing yourself **s a y** the words has been shown to reinforce memory retention. It is called auditory learning.

6.) **Visual Aids or Visual Association**- associate **k e y** words or phrases with visual or mental images. This is another proven way of memory retention.

7.) **Put Scripture to song**. Many people find it **e a s i e r** to memorize Scripture when they put the words to song.

8.) **Meditate on the Scripture verses daily**.
T h i n k about the verses and apply them to your life by obedience.

Joshua 1:8 *"This book of the law shall not depart out of thy mouth; but thou shalt meditate therein day and night, that thou mayest observe to do according to all that is written therein: for then thou shalt make thy way prosperous, and then thou shalt have good success."*

Appearance: What the unsaved see when they look at you.

2. **Attire**: Clothing forms a strong first impression. A doctor pays attention to attire. The President of the United States pays attention to attire. People will form an opinion of you simply by how you dress. As ambassadors for Christ, we should always be mindful of how we dress and that our attire reflects that we are Bible-believing Christians. Our attire does matter to God.

*2 Corinthians 5:20*a *"Now then we are ambassadors for Christ."*

    A. Clothing has played a significant role in the history of God's interaction with mankind from **Genesis 3:7** to **Revelation 22:14**.

    B. In many verses of the Bible, **o u t w a r d** attire symbolizes **i n w a r d** conditions, and clothing in many instances had spiritual significance.

    C. In the Bible certain clothing was worn to **d i s t i n g u i s h** who people were. Even today many lost people will use clothing to make a statement. Employees are required to wear certain clothing. In the Bible:

        1.) Kings would wear certain clothing.

        2.) Sackcloth was worn during mourning and times of grief.

        3.) Prostitutes in the Bible had a certain manner of dress.

        4.) Leather belts were a sign of poverty. Both Elijah and John the Baptist wore leather belts.

        5.) Deuteronomy 22:5 commands men not to wear female clothing and females not to wear men's clothing.

6.) Throughout the Bible white clothing has symbolized purity. At the Mount of Transfiguration, Jesus became as white as light. Those in God's kingdom in Revelation are seen in white clothing.

D. God's **e x p e c t a t i o n** on clothing is modesty and gender-appropriate clothing.

1.) The appearance of a soulwinner, a Christian, is important. BSALT recommends when going out for soulwinning outreach a "Business casual" dress for men, clean clothing of pants, a collared shirt, and comfortable shoes. For ladies, a modest dress or skirt, a conservative blouse, and comfortable shoes. Nothing about the attire should draw attention to the body.

2.) Every Christian should be clean and groomed. Consider your breath as well.

3. **Attitude**: A **b a d** or condescending attitude can be detrimental to winning the unsaved. Do not focus on their sin; they are not saved yet. They are following their sinful nature.

    A. Show them the **l o v e** of Christ.

    B. Show them the **j o y** of the Lord.

    C. Show them **k i n d n e s s** and friendship.

D. Never go soul-winning when you are in a bad mood, frustrated, or your attitude is not Christian-like. Your bad attitude can hinder not only your winning someone to Christ but could also hinder Christians in the future from winning them to Christ.

1.) **Never say anything negative** about someone you have visited during soulwinning. Your words can get around and a lot of damage can be done in leading that person to Christ.

2.) Remember what momma used to say,

a.) "Don't fly off the handle."

b.) "You better straighten up before I jerk a knot in you."

c.) "You are going to make me madder than a wet hen."

d.) "Can't never could."

e.) "You're cruising for a bruising."

f.) "Use your head for more than a hat rack."

g.) **"If you don't have anything nice to say, don't say anything at all."**

4. **Approach**: How you **a p p r o a c h** people is especially important.

   A. When you talk to someone, do not stand too close to them. **Personal space** refers to the physical and psychological space that individuals consider as their own and prefer to keep between themselves and others. Studies show that for most people this space is approximately 1.5 ft. to 4 ft.

   B. After you knock on someone's door to give them the gospel and an invitation, take a good **two steps back** (about 4-5 ft.). Many people do not want you too close to their front door.

   C. Wear a smile and be friendly.

   D. There are two answers that everyone wants to **k n o w** when you knock on their door.

      1.) Who are you?

      2.) What do you want?

      3.) The sooner you answer these two questions the better. The opening greeting should include something like this, "Hello I am _____. We are with _____ Baptist Church, and we would like to give you a personal invitation to come visit our church."

5. **Action:** Plan For Soul-Winning Outreach With Your Church

    A. Enjoy the journey! Learn as you go. Remember, what Jesus told his disciples in **Mark 1:17,** "... Come ye after me, and I will **make** you to become fishers of men."

    B. It takes time to learn to be a good soulwinner.

    C. Be consistent, be **involved**, and be faithful in obeying the Lord in personal soulwinning.

A Plan for Conversation

We have all had conversations with people at times, in which we get to talking and forget to talk about what we wanted to or came for. Sometimes when we want to witness to someone about the gospel, we will talk about everything but the gospel.

So, I want to give you an ACRONYMN to help you remember how to plan for the gospel conversation.

G **Greeting:**
Make a cordial greeting. Do not approach a home and walk through their flowers. When they answer the door or you meet someone in public, answer the two questions quickly. A cordial greeting sets the tone for the conversation. Nothing wrong with talking about the weather, vehicles, dogs, etc., but stay on track.

I **Invitation:**
Be sure to invite them to visit your church. Hand them an invitation or tract from your church. We have a motto with BSALT that **it takes two invitations to make a great invitation.** You may or may not get to share the gospel with them, but that is our goal.

V **Verbal exchange:**
This is the discussion. They may get defensive and not want to talk about the Lord. They may start asking you questions. They may tell you about their past or a testimony. They may take the conversation anywhere, but the key is to be a good listener.

Let their words and demeanor dictate how you proceed. You may or may not get to go any further but have discernment, and do not force the gospel. You have planted the seed already by giving them an invitation with the gospel message. However, if they are interested in more discussion, give them the gospel message verbally. Take the conversation as far as they are willing to go about the Lord Jesus Christ.

Do not forget that salvation must come from their heart and not yours. If they trust the Lord for salvation, be sure to leave them with assurance and the next steps.

E Make a cordial Exit:

Thank the person for their time. Let them know if they have any questions to give you a call. Maybe reiterate the invitation to come to visit the church. If they trust the Lord for salvation, let them know how happy you are for them. Always leave the door open for someone to water the seed. Do not forget to follow up.

Points To Ponder and Discuss:

1. Add Scripture to your memory.

2. Appearance is very important. It is what the unsaved see when they look at you.

    A. Attire: What you wear.

    B. Attitude: Your behavior can be seen very quickly.

    C. Approach: How you approach someone with the gospel makes a huge impact.

3. Action Plan: It takes time to become a good soul winner. Be consistent, involved, faithful, and obedient to the Lord in personal soulwinning.

4. A plan for conversation: G. I. V. E. acronym (Greeting, Invite, Verbal exchange, Exit)

LESSON EIGHT

STEALTH In Soul-Winning

We want to leave you with an Acronym to help you as you go out soulwinning with your church family. We strive to do this during our BSALT "Operations." STEALTH is a set of reminders when we go out and share the gospel.

S.T.E.A.L.T.H. reminds us to move forward and accomplish the objective of winning souls to Christ strategically, cautiously, and with an intentional approach. Always move forward!

S Safety

It is very important as Christians go out and share the gospel, especially door-to-door.

BSALT recommends:

1. Always keep your partner in view. Do not get separated; stay together.

2. On the initial outreach effort, do not go into the homes. Reserve this for follow-up visitation. Especially, never go into someone's home alone. In today's environment you do not have to be guilty of doing something wrong, just accused. It can destroy your testimony.

3. Watch out for dogs. If a sign on someone's fence says "Beware of dog," I would leave the invitation or bag on the fence. Do not **r i s k** getting bitten.

4. We recommend that if you have a ladies' team, always have a male team **c l o s e** by.

5. When engaging in door-to-door outreach, do not go out at night or too early in the morning.

6. Respect boundaries and privacy. If someone is not interested, then do not **p u s h** it.

7. Be alert and aware. Pay **a t t e n t i o n** to your surroundings.

8. Stay hydrated, take breaks, and carry snacks.

T Training
Roleplaying of possible discussions and questions. One thing that can build confidence in Christians to be soulwinners is discussing and roleplaying. This gives practice to our acronym of G.I.V.E. It also allows discussion of talking to people that hold to false religions such as the LDS and JW.

1. Learn to share your **t e s t i m o n y** (with your pastor, spouse, friend, or a mirror).

2. Practice sharing **S c r i p t u r e s** with someone (Roman's Road).

E Eternal Impact
Remember the **Eternal Impact** of what you are learning to do. There is no greater joy than leading someone to Christ and knowing that they will be with the Lord and you for all eternity because you gave them the gospel. What you are doing is an eternal work.

A Advantageous
Soulwinning is **advantageous to you**. The Lord Himself will reward us for our labor. Proverbs 11:30 tells us that it is wise to be a soulwinner. Daniel 12:13 tells us that those who turn people to righteousness will shine as the stars for eternity. 1 Thessalonians 2:19-20 reminds us there is a crown of rejoicing for bringing souls to Christ. Winning the lost to Jesus Christ is a very active way of laying up treasure in Heaven. It is to your advantage to win the lost.

L **Location**
Take some time before you go out soulwinning and know your locations. BSALT recommends having maps so that you can systematically reach neighborhoods house by house. Also, know what you should expect in your location. Is there a heavy Catholic presence? Is it a wealthy neighborhood or a high-crime area? Know your location and what you should expect.

T **Teamwork**
Working together is the best way to accomplish the objective of sharing the gospel. Work together with like-minded Christians.

"Coming together is a beginning. Keeping together is progress. Working together is success."

Henry Ford

If everyone is moving forward together, then success takes care of itself."

Henry Ford

1. The Great Commission implies a **c o l l e c t i v e** effort.

2. Jesus in **Mark 6:7** sent the disciples out **t w o** by two.

3. Jesus in **Mark 10:1** took the seventy and sent them out two by two.

4. The **team** plants and waters. ***1 Corinthians 3:6-9*** "For we are labourers together with God."

5. BSALT recommends going out two by two. Pair up a seasoned soulwinner, what we call the lead, with someone who is up and coming and learning. We call this person the silent partner. The lead person does the talking with the individual, and the silent partner provides materials and runs interference if there are distractions to the conversation. This is a great opportunity for the silent partner to watch, listen, and learn. Eventually, the silent partner should switch and get a chance to be the lead.

6. The goal of every Christian should be to become a seasoned soul winner who makes soul-winning a lifestyle and then teaches others to do the same.

H **Help**

Help is available for you to become a better soulwinner. Talk to your pastor about soulwinning and let him answer any questions you may have. Ask him for booklets or information you can read about soulwinning. The church will usually provide soul-winning materials for you to use to share the gospel.

Be Ready Always!!

1 Peter 3:15 *"But sanctify the Lord God in your hearts: and be* **r e a d y** *always to give an answer to every man that asketh you a reason of the hope that is in you with meekness and fear."*

"It is better to live ready than to get ready."

Unknown

"By failing to prepare, you are preparing to fail."

Benjamin Franklin

This is true when it comes to being a Christian. This is very true of being a soulwinner.

Christians should always be ready to give an answer for the hope that is in them (Why do you have hope?).

1. I have hope because I am saved. Be ready to give a testimony of your salvation.

2. I have hope because of the Bible's promise of salvation. Be ready to share those Scriptures.

3. We should always be ready. Practice makes ready.

4. There are two areas that many Christians are not ready to give an answer.

   A. A personal testimony of salvation

   B. Share Scriptures about salvation.

5. If not now, then when; if not you, then who?

On behalf of myself and the BSALT team, thank you for your interest in becoming a better soulwinner. Seasoned, dedicated soulwinners are a rarity in our day. Jesus reminds us of the importance and the need.

Luke 10:2 *Therefore said he unto them, The harvest truly is great, but the labourers are few: pray ye therefore the Lord of the harvest, that he would send forth labourers into his harvest.*

"I would rather win souls than be the greatest king or emperor on earth. I would rather win souls than be the greatest general that ever commanded an army. I would rather win souls than be the greatest poet or novelist or literary man who ever walked the earth. My one ambition in life is to win as many as possible."

R.A. Torrey

CONTACT INFORMATION:

Steven Sykes (BSALT Founder, Director)
Cell Phone: 505-916-7458

preacher1nm@gmail.com

The BSALT team is always in need of volunteers to help with soulwinning operations, material and literature development, and other communication needs. If you are interested in volunteering with the BSALT ministry, please discuss this with your pastor, and then give us a call. Together, we can make a greater difference.

Please pray for the BSALT ministry. If you would like to support BSALT financially, below is the address to send donations or a QR code in which you can give.

Thank you very much for your time, consideration, desire to see the lost saved, and for loving the Lord Jesus Christ.

Steven Sykes
BSALT Founder & Director
Church Planter in New Mexico

Support Address:
Southwestern Independent Baptist Clearinghouse (SIBC)
C/O BSALT
PO Box 25643
Albuquerque, NM 87125

Donate to BSALT
Through Cash App
$BSALT4SOULS

Made in the USA
Columbia, SC
21 February 2025